Cruisin' 4 Fun!
A Kid's Guide To Santa Cruz, California

Photography By John D. Weigand
Poetry By Penelope Dyan

Bellissima Publishing, LLC
Jamul, California
www.bellissimapublishing.com

Copyright © 2013 by Penny D. Weigand and John D. Weigand

All rights reserved. No part of this book may be reproduced or transmitted in any form or by any means, electronic or mechanical, including photocopying, recording, or by any other means, or by any information or storage retrieval system, without permission from the publisher.

ISBN 978-1-61477-082-4
First Edition

"To myself I am only a child playing on the beach, while vast oceans of truth lie undiscovered before me."

ISAAC NEWTON

Cruisin' 4 Fun!
Bellissima Publishing, LLC

Introduction

Santa Cruz, California is an extremely fun place to visit. There are miles of Sandy Beaches, a roller coaster that seems to go up and down and on and on forever, bicycles you can ride, a long wharf with shopping and restaurants where it only costs a buck to park for 4 hours, the wonderful Seymour Marine Discovery Center, and more--This list doesn't even include the University of California at Santa Cruz! Of course, this beach town is close to Monterey, and part of Santa Cruz faces the Monterey Bay where (in Monterey, California) you can visit the great Monterey Bay Aquarium and see sea otters. Just up in the mountains you can visit and ride the Roaring Camp Railroad where you can take a ride on train driven by an 1800's steam locomotive and see a part of the great redwood forest, which is also the subject of another great Bellissima book, 'The Comeback Kids, Book 12, The Redwood Forest.' If you are noticing a theme of fun and learning at Bellissima Publishing, LLC, then you are quite correct!

Written by award winning author, attorney and former teacher, Penelope Dyan, with Photographs by John D. Weigand, this book is meant strictly for kids. This book is what kids love to do and see, and about what catches the eyes of a child. Use this book in conjunction with the other Bellissima tools, such as the music video on the Bellissimavideo YouTube channel.

Cruisin' 4 Fun!
Bellissima Publishing, LLC

Cruisin' 4 Fun!
A Kid's Guide To Santa Cruz, California

Photography By John D. Weigand
Poetry By Penelope Dyan

There is a lighthouse standing
proud and tall.
It's been given a new use
as a 'Surfing Museum,' after all.
If you go in for a big explore,
you will find that inside
there is even more!

There is a roller coaster
and a beach where you can swim,
and you wonder where you
should even begin.

You drive up the wharf, park, go inside and take a seat, where you sit down and have something to eat.

And from the wharf
you take in the view,
because it seems like it's
the thing to do.
You want to get over there
and in the sun play,
because for fun it's a perfect day!

But first you go to see
the bones of a gray whale,
as your dad recites something
from the 'Moby Dick' tale.

A rusty old anchor lays on a curb right next to your feet.
Your dad thinks that is really neat!

You're finally at the
Seymour Marine Discovery Center,
ready to go inside.
Right next to where you are headed,
the bones of a blue whale reside!
You stop and take a good long look.
This is an experience
you can't get from a book!

People surround
an elephant seal statue.
Listening carefully to a guide,
they all stand.
Your mom whispers, "You get to do
some hands on stuff inside."
And you whisper back,
"Wow! That's really grand!"

You see a little girl examine the wood chips in her hand.

As your memory reflects back
to those beaches,
and those miles and miles
of blue water and sand.

And you wonder if you happen
to go up
in that roller coaster oh so high,
if you will be able to
reach right out and touch
the blue of that sunny
Santa Cruz, California sky!

You wonder if later you will drive to
see the redwood forest.
(You can get there in your car.)
It is just up in the mountains,
and it's NOT very far.
Your head is really in a spin!
There is so much fun ahead,
you just don't know where to begin!
Your mom says,
"We'll stay here at the beach today.
Tomorrow we'll see the redwoods
and ride the steam train and play!"
Your face bursts into a big, big smile.
(You suspected THIS all the while!)

"Where does a wise man kick a pebble? On the beach.
Where does a wise man hide a leaf? In the forest."

G. K. Chesterton

www.ingramcontent.com/pod-product-compliance
Ingram Content Group UK Ltd.
Pitfield, Milton Keynes, MK11 3LW, UK
UKHW060132240426
12048UKWH00002B/12